Ready-made playful pom-poms are easy to add to all kinds of projects. Simply attach with hot glue or string them onto a thread, wire, or nylon line. Make each project unique by choosing your favorite colors or adapting the ideas to other objects.

LEISURE ARTS, INC. • Maumelle, Arkansas

LAMPSHADE

SHOPPING LIST

- lampshade (ours measures $8^1/_4$" high with a $9^1/_4$" diameter at the bottom edge)
- $^1/_2$" wide ribbon (we used $1^5/_8$ yards)*
- pink pom-pom trim (we used $1^5/_8$ yards)*
- hot glue gun and glue sticks

* See Step 1 to measure for yardage if your lampshade is a different size.

To make the Lampshade:

1. To determine yardage for ribbon and pom-pom trim, measure the circumference of the top and bottom edges of your shade; add 2" to each measurement. Add the top and bottom measurements together for the total number of inches needed. For yardage, divide the inches by 36.

2. From pom-pom trim, cut a length the top edge measurement. Cut a length the bottom edge measurement. Repeat to cut top and bottom lengths from ribbon.

3. Beginning and ending at the center back and overlapping ends by about 1", glue the pom-pom trim around the top edge of the lampshade. Repeat to glue pom-pom trim around the bottom edge.

4. Repeat Step 3 to glue the ribbon lengths over the pom-pom trim.

RUG

Finished size: 18" x 24"

SHOPPING LIST

- approximately 100 2" diameter multi-color pom-poms
- approximately 120 1½" diameter multi-color pom-poms
- 2 12" x 18" 7-mesh plastic canvas sheets
- heavy-duty sewing thread and a large sewing needle
- wax paper
- hot glue gun and glue sticks

To make the Rug:

1. To make the base, match long edges and place the plastic canvas sheets side by side. With the thread doubled and working in adjacent holes, stitch the sheets together along the length ***(Fig. 1)***.

Fig. 1

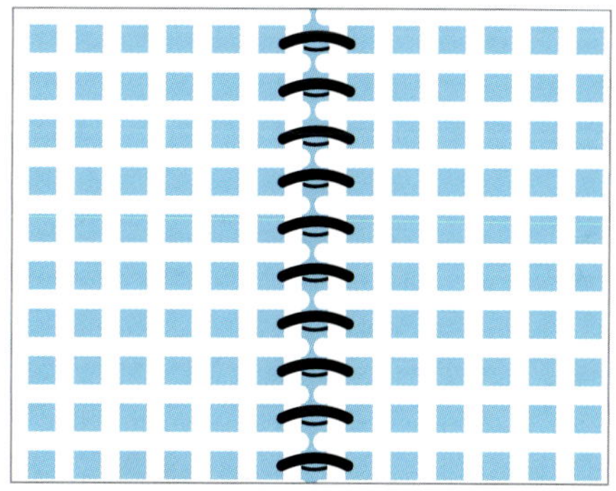

2. Cover your work area with wax paper. Starting at one corner, glue a row of assorted pom-poms across one edge of the base.

3. Continue adding rows of pom-poms until the base is covered. Check for any bare areas by running your hand across the surface of the rug. Fill in with additional pom-poms, if needed.

HEADBANDS

For a quick upgrade to a plain headband, use hot glue to adhere a single row of brightly-colored, extra-large pom-poms to a headband.

For a slightly different, but equally easy look, decorate a headband with multiple rows of small pom-poms. No matter which look you choose, you are sure to turn heads.

HAIR CLIPS

Quick, easy, and so inexpensive to make, these colorful hair ornaments make great gifts or party favors.

Embellish plain barrettes and hair clips with pom-poms and hot glue! Cover a barrette with a rainbow of small pom-poms. For the hairclips, glue a single medium pom-pom or a trio of mini pom-poms to the end of a clip.

NECKLACE
& BRACELET

SHOPPING LIST

- 23 blue 1/2" diameter pom-poms
- 2 yards of gold large link chain
- 25 6mm gold jump rings
- 23 gold head pins
- 2 gold magnetic clasps
- round-nose pliers
- chain-nose pliers (2 pair)
- wire cutters

To make the Necklace:

1. Cut one 26" and one 22" length of chain. With the shorter chain to the inside and the ends even, arrange the chains in a U shape on your work surface. Use the chain-nose pliers to attach both chain ends on one side of the U to a jump ring *(Fig. 1)*. Attach the remaining chain ends to a second jump ring. Attach 1 clasp piece to each jump ring.

Fig. 1

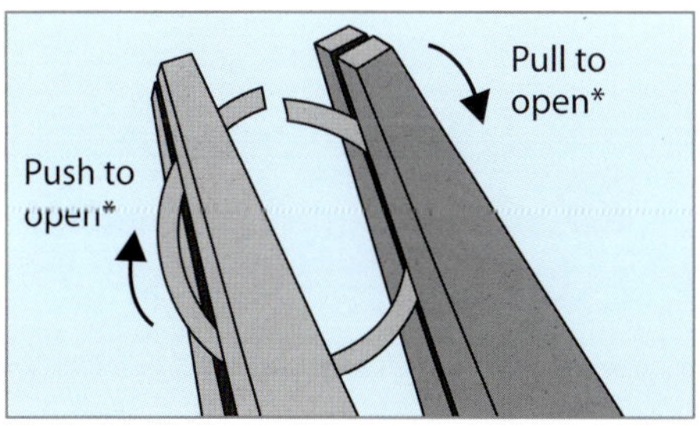

*Do the opposite to close.

2. To make a pom-pom dangle, thread 1 pom-pom on a head pin. Leaving about 1/2", cut off the excess wire. Using chain-nose pliers, bend the wire at a 90° angle ***(Fig. 2)***. Grasp the wire end with the round-nose pliers. Turn the pliers, bending the end into a loop ***(Figs. 3-4)***. Release the pliers. Straighten or twist the loop further if necessary. Make 23 pom-pom dangles. Set 5 dangles aside for the bracelet.

Fig. 2

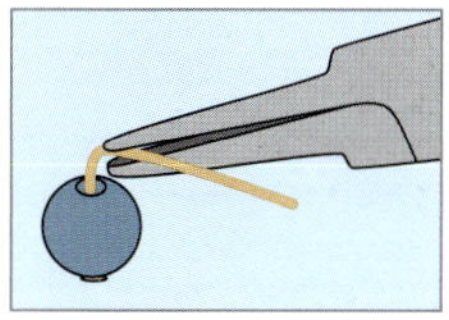

Fig. 3

Fig. 4

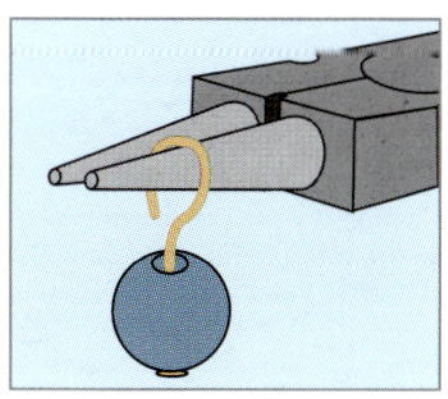

3. Find the center of the shorter chain and use a jump ring to attach a dangle to the center link. Spacing 1" apart, add 3 more dangles to each side of the center. Repeat on the longer chain, adding 5 dangles to either side of the center.

To make the Bracelet:

1. Measure your wrist and decide how loose or tight you want your bracelet; subtract 3/4" for the clasp and jump rings. Cut 2 lengths of chain this measurement. With the chains even, attach two ends of the chains to a jump ring ***(Fig. 1)***. Attach the remaining chain ends to a second jump ring. Attach 1 clasp piece to each jump ring.

2. Use a jump ring to attach a dangle to the center link of one chain. Spacing 2" apart, add a dangle to either side of the center. On the remaining chain, attach a dangle 1" from either side of the center.

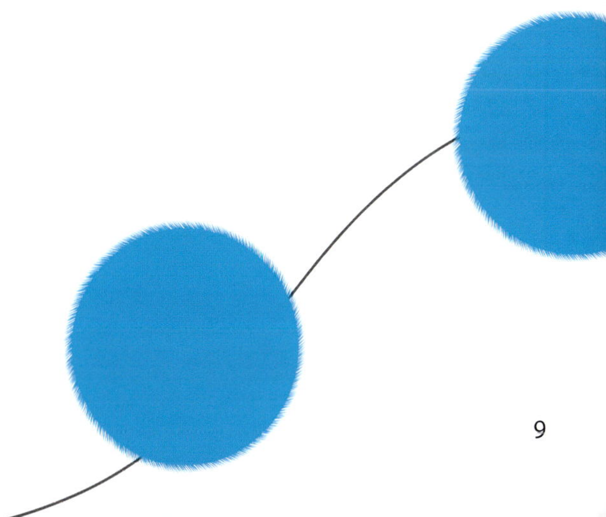

MOBILE

Finished size: 8" x 30"

SHOPPING LIST

- 3 8" diameter wood embroidery hoops*
- approximately 35 assorted 1/2" - 2" diameter pom-poms
- blue acrylic paint and paintbrush
- nylon fishing line and a large-eye hand sewing needle
- needle-nose pliers (optional)
- hot glue and glue sticks

*You will only use the inner rings of the embroidery hoops.

To make the Mobile:

1. Paint the rings blue; allow to dry. Place the rings inside of each other and arrange them in a sphere shape; glue in place.

2. Cut 5 26" lengths of fishing line. Make a knot in one end of each length; apply glue to each knot and allow to dry.

3. Use the needle to string 7 pom-poms on each length. If the pom-poms tend to slide down the line, apply a small amount of glue to the line just under the pom-pom.

Tip: Using needle-nose pliers to help pull the needle through the dense center of the pom-poms makes stringing the pom-poms easier.

4. Spacing as desired, tie the pom-pom lengths to the ring assembly. Apply glue to each knot and allow to dry; trim excess line close to the knot.

5. To hang, tie a loop of fishing line to the top of the ring assembly.

Laura Moriarty

LOVE

Finished size: 15" x 5"

SHOPPING LIST

- 15" x 5" LOVE wood sign
- approximately 60 $\frac{3}{4}$" diameter dark blue pom-poms
- approximately 60 $\frac{3}{4}$" diameter aqua pom-poms
- aqua acrylic paint and paintbrush
- sandpaper
- hot glue gun and glue sticks

To make the Love Sign:

1. Sand the sign to smooth away any rough areas. Paint the sign aqua; allow to dry.

2. Alternating colors, glue the pom-poms to the sign.

CUFF BRACELET

SHOPPING LIST

- wide ribbon (we used 1 7/8" wide woven ribbon)
- sew-on magnetic snaps
- 3/8" or 1/2" diameter pom-poms
- embroidery floss and a large-eye needle
- water-or air-soluble fabric marker

To make the Bracelet:

1. Measure around your wrist and add 3" to this measurement. Cut a length of ribbon this measurement.

2. Turn each short ribbon end 1/4" to the wrong side twice; pin.

3. Thread the needle with an 18" length of embroidery floss; knot one end. With the knot on the wrong side and going through all layers, use 1/8" long stitches to hem one short end; knot off and trim floss close to the knot. Repeat on the remaining short end ***(Fig. 1)***.

Fig. 1

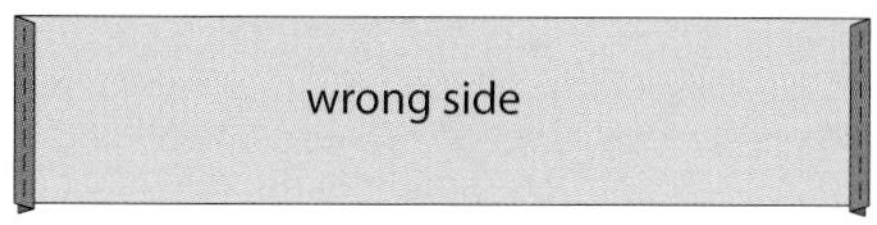

4. Thread the needle with a 24" length of embroidery floss; knot one end. Starting on one long edge with the knot on the wrong side, bring the needle to the right side. Thread a pom-pom on the needle and slide it down the floss stopping about 1/2" from the ribbon. Leaving the 1/2" slack in the floss, bring the needle to the wrong side of the ribbon and make 2 1/4" long running stitches. Repeat across the length of the bracelet; knot off and trim floss close to the knot. Repeat on the remaining long side ***(Fig. 2)***.

Fig. 2

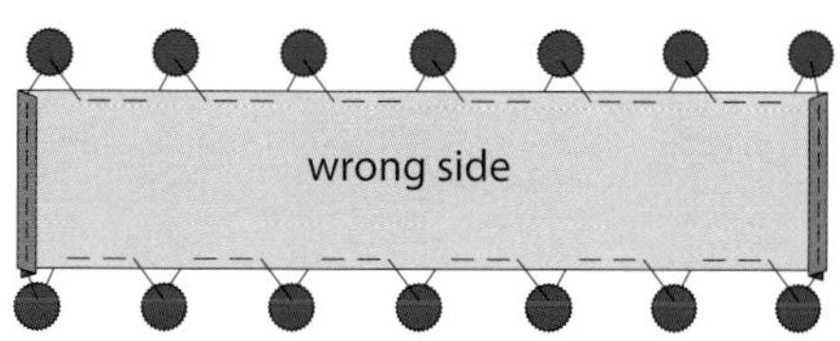

5. On the wrong side, sew the 2 female snap pieces close to one short end ***(Fig. 3)***.

Fig. 3

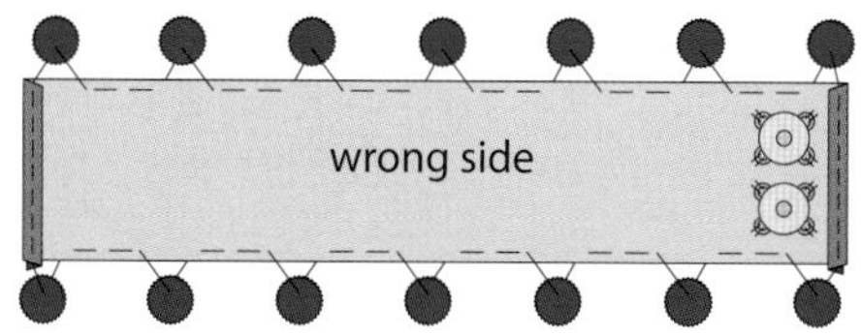

6. Overlapping short ends, wrap the bracelet around your wrist to determine a comfortable fit. Use the fabric marker to mark the placement of the remaining snap pieces on the right side of the bracelet. Sew one snap piece at each mark ***(Fig. 4)***.

Fig. 4

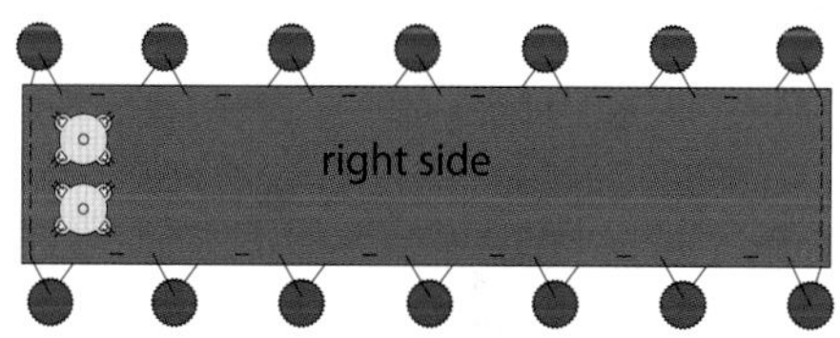

CLIP-ON DANGLES

Make a statement when you clip a pom-pom dangle or two to a favorite purse. Made from wooden beads and giant pom-poms, these dangles add a touch of glam to an otherwise mundane black purse.

SHOPPING LIST

- assorted wood beads
- 2" diameter pom-poms
- 3" diameter fake fur pom-poms
- swivel clips
- nylon fishing line
- large-eye sewing needle
- craft glue

To make one Dangle:

1. Cut an 18" length of fishing line. Tie a double knot in one end of the line; thread the other end through the needle.

2. Thread a 3" diameter pom-pom, a 2" diameter pom-pom, and assorted wood beads on the line until the dangle is the desired length.

3. Tie the dangle to a swivel clip; tie a second knot. Place a drop of glue on the knot and allow to dry; trim excess line close to the knot. Clip the dangle to a purse.

Tip: Using needle-nose pliers to help pull the needle through the dense center of the pom-poms makes stringing the pom-poms easier.

BEACH BAG

Want to make your beach bag stand out from the rest? Just use hot glue to adhere 3 jumbo, pom-poms to each side of a straw tote and you are ready to hit the sand!

Keep your bag traditional with neutral-color pom-poms, pick pom-pom colors to match your swim suit, or mix it up with multi-color pom-poms that will blend with any outfit!

DRY-ERASE CALENDAR

Transform a boring magnetic dry-erase wall calendar into an enticing family command center with the addition of brightly-colored pom-poms around the edge of the frame.

A little hot glue and a lot of 1/2" diameter pom-poms is all it takes. Add some colorful magnets for holding notes and the entire family will be heading to the board to leave messages and view upcoming activities.

SANDALS

With the addition of brightly-colored ribbons and pom-poms these formerly plain white sandals will become your go-to summer shoes.

Simply measure the width of the straps and purchase about a 1/2 yard of three assorted grosgrain ribbons that are just a little narrower than the strap width (we used 3/8" wide ribbon on 1/2" wide straps). Use hot glue to adhere the ribbon to the straps; add assorted pom-poms and you are finished!

And...you don't have to stop with sandals! Do you have a tired, but comfy, pair of flats? Glue ribbon and pom-poms around the top edge and across the toe. Make your workouts more fun by adding ribbon and pom-pom stripes to the sides of your athletic shoes!

POM-POM FLOWER

SHOPPING LIST

- assorted sizes and colors of pom-poms from 1/8" to 2" diameter
- 18" long 18-gauge green cloth floral stems
- wine bottle (ours is 12" high)
- aqua chalk paint and a paintbrush
- jute twine
- hot glue gun and glue sticks
- needle-nose pliers
- wire cutters (optional) *

To make the Flowers:

1. Flower 1 (white spray). Slide 9 1" diameter pom-poms onto a floral stem. Use the pliers to bend the top 1/4" of the stem over until it touches the stem. To keep the pom-poms from sliding apply a small amount of glue above and below the first and last pom-poms.

2. Flowers 2 (yellow, blue, and lavender large single buds). For each flower, glue a large or extra large pom-pom to the end of a floral stem.

3. Flower 3 (green spray). Start at the top and work down to glue 20 1/2" pom-poms, spaced about 1/2" apart, to opposite sides of a stem.

4. Flowers 4 (lavender, yellow, and pink clusters). For the lavender flower, glue a medium pom-pom to the end of a stem; completely cover the pom-pom with same color small pom-poms. Repeat for the pink and yellow flowers using a small pom-pom as the base and covering it with tiny pom-poms. Glue two pom-pom "leaves" to each stem.

To make the Vase:

1. Remove any labels; wash and dry the bottle. Paint the bottle aqua; allow to dry.

2. Starting about 1/2" below the rim at the back of the bottle, glue 1 end of the jute twine to the bottle neck. Gluing as needed at the back, tightly wrap the jute around the bottle neck for about 2" or a length that best fits your bottle. Cut the jute and glue the end to the bottle.

3. Arrange the flowers in the vase; add extra height* to some stems, if desired.

* To make some of the flowers taller, we cut 4"-8" lengths of floral stems and attached them to the flower stems by twisting the ends together. If using a shorter bottle, you may not need additional height.

WREATH

Finished size:
approximately 13" diameter

SHOPPING LIST

- approximately 100 assorted 1/2" - 2" diameter pom-poms (white)
- 7-8 1/2" diameter pom-poms (white glitter)
- 7-8 1/2" diameter pom-poms (silver glitter)
- 12" x 12" piece of white foam core board
- 1 yard of 3mm silver braid
- 1 yard of 2 1/2" wide silver ribbon
- hot glue gun and glue sticks

To make the Wreath:

1. To make the wreath base, cut a 12" diameter circle from foam core board. Cut a 6 1/2" diameter circle from the center of the 12" circle.

2. Glue the white pom-poms to the wreath base. Spacing as desired, glue the silver and white glitter pom-poms to the wreath.

3. Glue one end of the braid to the wrong side of the wreath base. Wrap the wreath with the braid; glue the remaining end to the wrong side of the wreath base.

4. Tie the ribbon into a bow. Glue the bow to the wreath; trim ends into an upside down V.

GARLAND

When party time rolls around, be sure to include this festive Garland in your decorations.

Determine the length you want your garland and add 12"; cut a length of light-weight white cotton crochet thread or string this measurement.

Use a sharp, large-eye needle to string as many assorted size pom-poms as you like along the length of the thread. To hang, tie a 3" loop at each end of the garland.

Tip: Using needle-nose pliers to help pull the needle through the dense center of the pom-poms makes stringing your garland a breeze.

FRAME

SHOPPING LIST

- wood picture frame
- assorted 1/2" - 2" diameter pom-poms (lavender, purple, and white)
- acrylic paint (white and purple)
- paintbrush
- sandpaper
- hot glue gun and glue sticks

To make the Frame:

Always allow paint to dry between applications.

1. Sand the frame to smooth away any rough areas.
2. Paint the frame white. Paint the frame purple.
3. Sand away some of the purple paint, allowing the white to show through.
4. Working from largest to smallest, glue assorted pom-poms to the top right and bottom left corners of the frame.

PARTY HATS

Adding a personal touch to a child's party can be as simple as gluing pom-poms and pom-pom trim to purchased party hats. For a one-of-a kind look, start from scratch to make and decorate the hats.

SHOPPING LIST

- ready-made party hats ***or*** cardstock (one $8\frac{1}{2}$" x 11" sheet for each hat)
- optional pom-pom trim (approximately 13" for each hat)
- $1\frac{1}{2}$" diameter pom-poms (one for each hat)
- elastic cord
- $\frac{1}{8}$" diameter hole punch
- tracing paper
- hot glue gun and glue sticks

To make one Hat:

1. To decorate a ready-made hat, skip to Step 4. To make the hat, trace the hat pattern, below, onto tracing paper; cut out. Use the pattern to cut a hat from cardstock.

2. Overlapping the long straight edges about 1/4" at the center back, roll the cardstock into a cone; glue the overlapped edges together.

3. Punch a hole about 1/4" from the bottom edge on each side of the hat. Thread one end of a 14" elastic cord length through each hole; knot.

4. Measure around the bottom edge of the hat and add 1"; cut a length of pom-pom trim this measurement. Overlapping at the center back, glue the trim around the bottom edge. Glue a pom-pom to the top of the hat.

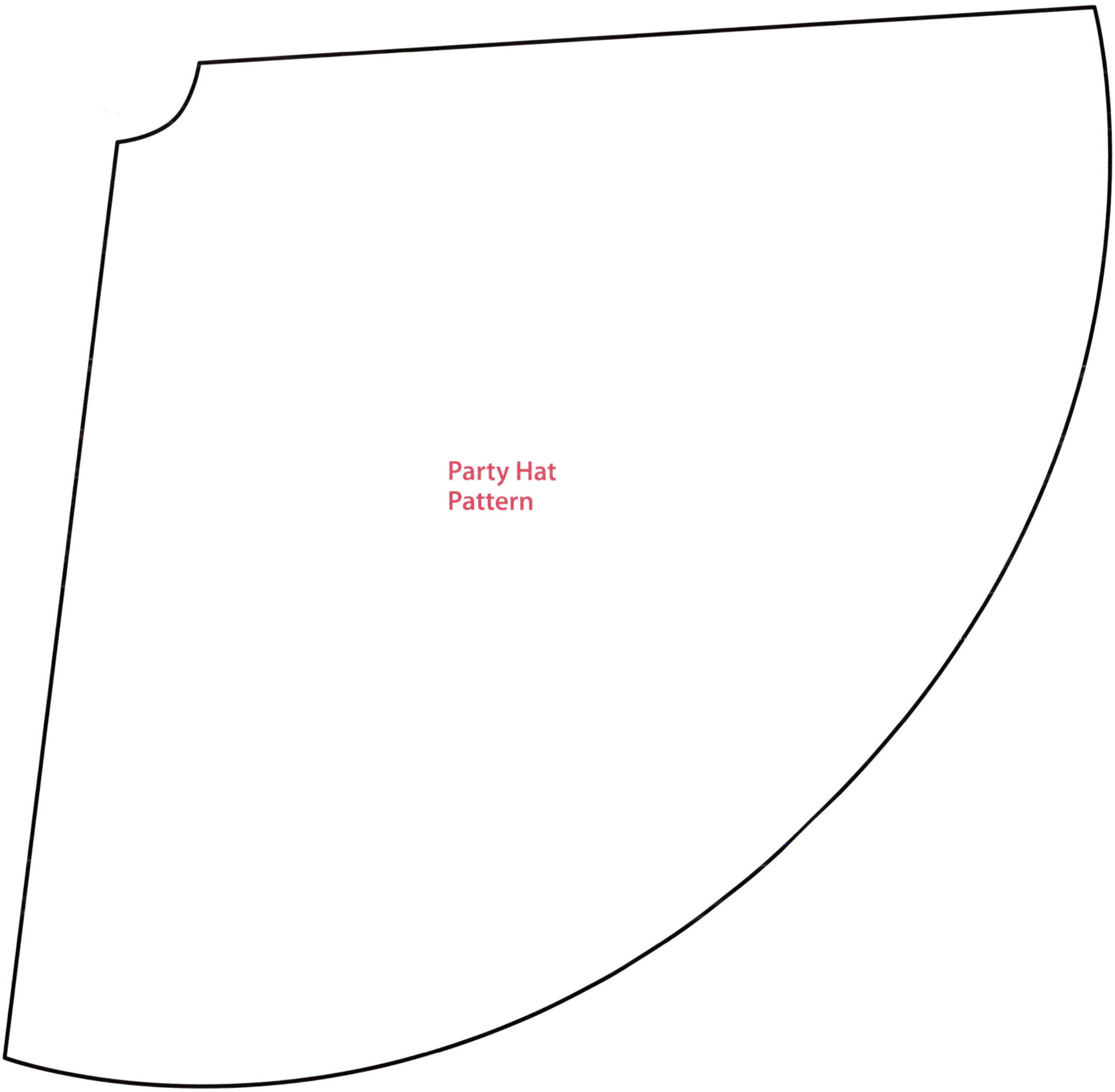

SHOPPING LIST

- $^{1}/_{2}$ yard of white/silver dot fabric
- 92 $^{1}/_{2}$" diameter black pom-poms
- 28 $^{3}/_{4}$" diameter white pom-poms
- white general purpose thread and a hand sewing needle
- polyester fiberfill
- wax paper
- clear tape
- chopstick or knitting needle (for pushing out corners)
- hot glue gun and glue sticks

HELLO PILLOW

Finished size
20" x 12"

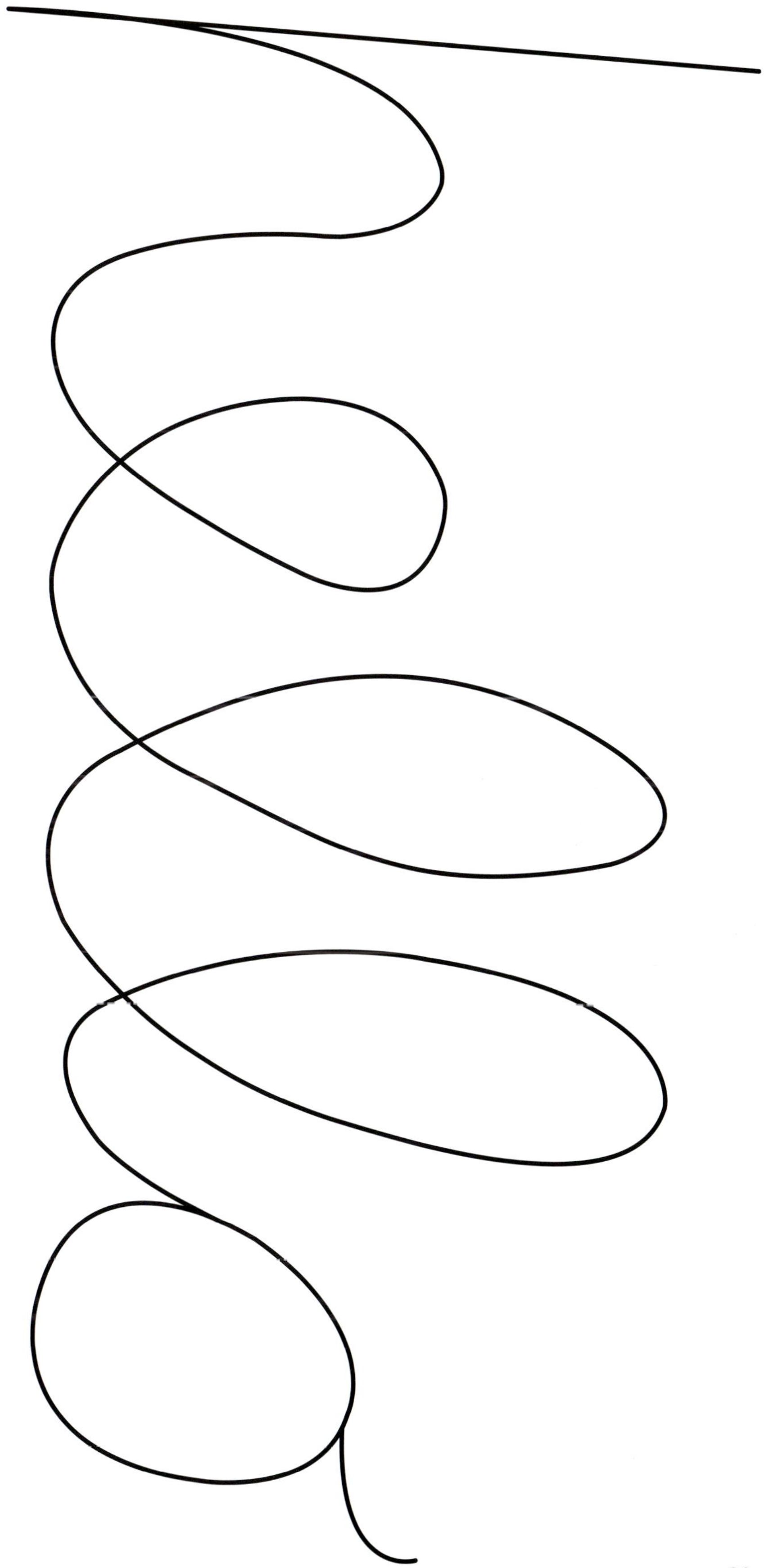

To make the Pillow:

Match right sides and use a $\frac{1}{4}$" seam allowance.

1. Cut 2 rectangles $20\frac{1}{2}$" x $12\frac{1}{2}$" from fabric. Leaving a 5" opening along one long edge for turning and stuffing, sew the rectangles together; clip corners. Turn right side out and use a chopstick or knitting needle to carefully push out the corners; press.

2. Make a photocopy of the "hello" pattern, right; trim the paper to 11" x 7". Cut a piece of wax paper the same size; tape the wax paper over the pattern. Insert the pattern into the pillow; center and pin.

3. Following the pattern, glue black pom-poms to the pillow front. Remove the pattern. Firmly stuff the pillow with fiberfill. Folding the raw edges to the wrong side, hand sew the opening closed.

4. Sew one white pom-pom to each pillow corner. Spacing about every two inches, sew white pom-poms along each seam.

TIEBACK

SHOPPING LIST

- 2 yards **each** of white and aqua 5mm twisted cord
- 2½ yards of grey 5mm twisted cord
- 2 1½" diameter white pom-poms
- 2 2" diameter white pom-poms
- 2 3" diameter white pom-poms
- clear tape
- hot glue gun and glue sticks

To make one Tieback:

When cutting or trimming cord, wrap the section to be cut with clear tape. Make the cut in the center of the tape.

1. Cut an 18" length from grey cord; set aside.

2. Holding the 2 yard cords together at one end, tape the ends to your work surface. Measure down the cords about 10" and glue the cords together at the 10" mark.

3. Braid the cords ***(Figs. 1-2)*** for 24". Glue the cords together close to the end of the braid.

Fig. 1

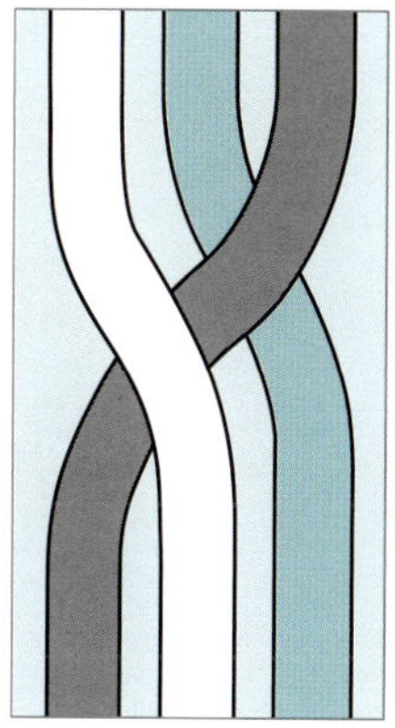

Fig. 2

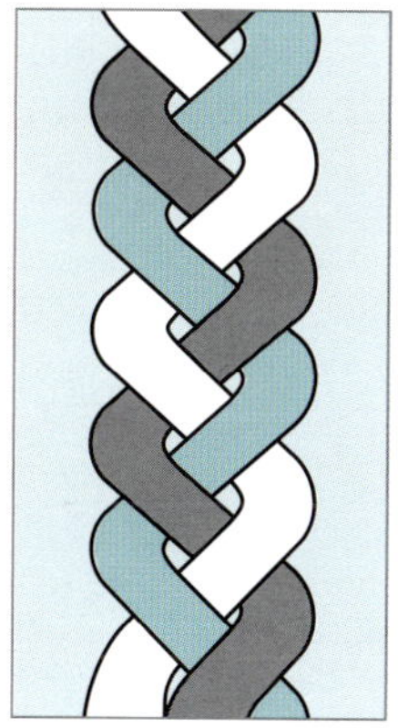

4. Form the braid into a loop with about 1½" of the unbraided section overlapped ***(Fig. 3);*** glue to hold the cords in place. Starting and ending on the wrong (back) side, wrap and glue the 18" cord around about 1½" of the overlapped cords; trim any excess grey cord.

Fig. 3

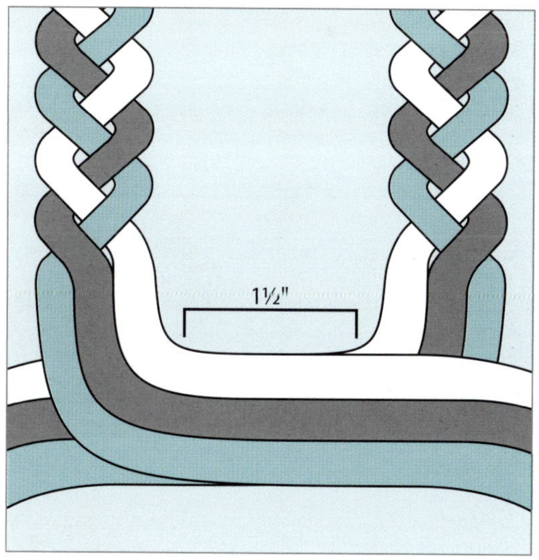

5. Trim the grey cord tails to 6", the white cord tails to 8", and the aqua cord tails to 8". Glue a 1½" pom-pom to each aqua cord end, a 2" pom-pom to each grey cord end, and a 3" pom-pom to each white cord end.

MEET MONICA SEAGRAVE

The simple love of making beautiful things is what drives Monica Seagrave to craft and paint.

"My favorite projects consist of taking something that looks outdated or unusable and making it into something current and lovely," she says.

"I have no formal training and very minimal experience. I just see something or think of something and it sort of comes natural to me."

Monica and her husband live in central Arkansas with their 2-year-old daughter and two cats. "I have a day job making people happy at Edible Arrangements, but in my spare time, I love crafting, painting, reading, and playing with my daughter."

Production Team: Technical Writer – Jean Lewis; Technical Associate – Lisa Lancaster; Editorial Writer – Susan Frantz Wiles; Senior Graphic Artist – Lora Puls; Graphic Artist – Kellie McAnulty; Photostylist – Lori Wenger; Photographer – Jason Masters.

Made in U.S.A.